Flowers of the Heavens

Poems

Praise for *Flowers of the Heavens*

"I've been dragging an old bag / of Southern through the years," Joyce Compton Brown tells us in the opening poem in her new collection, *Flowers of the Heavens*. We are enriched and enthralled by this bag's slow unpacking. Brown's insightful, image-laden poems from and about the rural South avoid simple nostalgia by their careful attention to the surprising detail and their willingness to look critically at the past and its legacy. They offer us views through the lenses of botany, history, foodways, and art, to name just a few—even the mule of a long dead neighbor becomes part of this collective memory "illuminating the frail / and certain paths" of Brown's native region.

—Pauletta Hansel, author of *Heartbreak Tree*, winner of the Poetry Society of Virginia's 2023 North American Book Award

Joyce Compton Brown's new poetry collection *Flowers of the Heavens* evokes memories without relying on sentimentality, such as what to do with neglected quilting frames, an old Jesus print, and movingly, the unresolved loss of dear people and places. These reflections of value come with sly humor, wit, and unexpected allusions to figures like Anne Bradstreet and Ezra Pound. Never nostalgic, consistently thoughtful, Brown's work offers inviting considerations of how we decide what we hold on to.

—Thomas Alan Holmes, author of *In the Backhoe's Shadow*

Here the reader will enjoy Joyce Compton Brown's masterful skill in the forms ghazal and duplex and sonnet, among wildly free narrative poems which tell the history of Appalachian North Carolina, the history of a woman's family and travels, the history of her education and experience. There is an acknowledgment of grief and even the brutality of loss. But the speaker declares the marvel of this collection: "you'd think it might carry / a bitter taste from all those years / of history." No. These poems have not one tinge of bitterness, nor are they blind to the fact that the poet has had a long life, outliving most of her kin and peers. These poems are such a gift of resilience and wisdom, shining the absolute richest patina while sharing the most profound details of an observed life. This is a book of lullabies about tragedies. We are soothed and swaddled, but the truth "of raw survival" is the haunting melody. Here the poet declares, "We know our grief by things our loved ones touched." Every delicate, loving touch comes to life in these moving and transcendent poems.

—Susan O'Dell Underwood, author
of *Splinter* and *Genesis Road*

Joyce Compton Brown is a poet of a particular place, people, time, and of a woman's perspective. In *Flowers of the Heavens*, her poetic voice achieves its fullest, most fearless expression. The book's intentions are made clear in the first poem, "A Slow Unpacking." "I've been dragging an old bag / of Southern through the years." The grandfathers' "spiteful gray uniforms," "the easy naïveté / of a small town," "racism, that unchangeable fact," old churches, love of land, the evil of poll taxes, home-churned ice cream—"all in that burdensome / bag of old joys, sorrows, and regrets…" The unpacking reveals, through the vehicle of tightly crafted, sonorously satisfying poetry, the heavy work of women, the inner lives of children living on the edge of poverty, a young family burdened by loss and grief, and, in the poet's later years, the grief of the surviving sibling. Poems about contemporary losses of traditional ways for easier ways, of farmland and forested land for development and profit ring with righteous anger. The natural world seems alive in these pages, closely observed from a lifetime of cherishing. "I offer back porch / benediction" is Brown's blessing on the fully realized world she offers to the reader in these pages.

—Joan Barasovska, author of *Orange Tulips*

Also by Joyce Compton Brown:

Poetry

Hard-Packed Clay (2022)
Standing on the Outcrop (2021)
Singing with Jarred Edges (2018)
Bequest (2015)

Flowers of the Heavens

Poems

Joyce Compton Brown

Lake Dallas, Texas

Copyright © 2025 by Joyce Compton Brown
All rights reserved
Printed in the United States of America

FIRST EDITION

Requests for permission to reprint or reuse material
from this work should be sent to:

Permissions
Madville Publishing
PO Box 358
Lake Dallas, TX 75065

Cover Design: Kimberly Davis
Cover Art: Vincent van Gogh, *Irises*, 1889, Oil on canvas.
The J. Paul Getty Museum, Los Angeles.

Author Photo: Les Brown

ISBN: 978-1-963695-37-3 paperback
978-1-963695-38-0 ebook
Library of Congress Control Number: 2024943522

In memory of my mother,
Vera Troutman Compton, who read to me.

Contents

I.

1	A Slow Unpacking
2	Passionflowers
4	The Liturgy of Chores
6	Chinaberry Tree
8	My Neighbor Deals with Her Robert E. Lee Painting
9	In the Tax Collector's Office
10	Afternoons in the Neighborhood
12	Miss Reese
13	Ceremonial
15	After Her Departure
16	Musicality
17	Oatmeal
19	Hog Pen Seasons
20	Home Economics
21	Pinto Beans

II.

25	Years
26	Black Swallowtail, New Birthed
27	Stitching
29	What We Carry
30	Translucent
31	Saturdays
32	Spider Lilies
33	Faucet
35	My Brother Takes a Paper Route
36	Winter Studies
37	Warped
39	Old Women Passing Time
40	Thanksgiving Day
41	Morning in the Cove

42	Searching for My Brother
44	Spawning Fish Against the Dam
45	First Iris

III.

49	Royal Purple
51	Duplex for Junk Mail
52	Sunday Evening
53	Photo of Boy and Dog: Triptych
55	Ghazal for the Lost
56	Surfacing the Swamp
57	For an Unknown Father
58	Road
59	Lake Walk in January
60	Instructions for a Winter Day
61	About the Old Jesus Print Propped Up Behind the Chest in My Bedroom
62	Pompeii
63	Butterfly Weed
64	Monuments
65	Apology to Ralph's Mule
67	My Mother Digs Up Irises When She Moves
68	Eclipse with Bees
70	Watching the Rain
71	Last Light
72	Notes
73	Acknowledgments
75	About the Author

I.

You don't love because: you love despite; not for its virtues, but despite its faults.

—William Faulkner

A Slow Unpacking

I've been dragging an old bag
of Southern through the years—
all those grandfathers, some with the spiteful
gray uniform—mothers, with their recipes
for reunion days, the easy naiveté
of a small town—Neil's Grocery and Poole's
Dime—where I learned to make change
and was taught racism, that unchangeable fact.

And these old churches,
town cornerstones, the stiff Lutheran
one, packed with lists of don'ts,
but spilling forth sweet harmony
in roiling tunes. Teetotaler weddings
with Kool-Aid punch and butter mints
underlaid by good moonshine stories
of my German grandfathers—

their pride, their love of land, their greed.
Grandmothers bearing too many children
for working the farm, cooking, canning,
tending the garden till they dropped.
Mine is a too-pale Southernness—
pale mayors, sheriffs, and county registrars,
where tax officers charged two dollars
for a Black man to vote if he didn't own land.
And how could he possibly own land?

And still I speak with dropped g's and extra r's,
icons of my roots. But oh, ice cream churns
and watermelons cracking open on the front
porch and county fairs and lightning bugs,
reunions, country fried steak, and my mother's
chocolate pie—all in that burdensome
bag of old joys, sorrows, and regrets
brimming with forgiveness and hope.

Passionflowers

Mollypops, we called them, stomping
with our small shoes.
We heaved them like baseballs,
burst them green
against the barn wall.
We were children, seeking
to destroy, as children do,
leaving the juice-encased seeds
to rot, perhaps reseed the pasture's edge.

Now I watch them in the garden.
They droop egg-like,
ripen toward yellow,
drape palmate leaves
like mittened hands
sheltering blossom and fruit.
How frail the flowers perched
atop the leaves, a few
still blooming purple!

Passiflora incarnata,
naked as Botticelli's Chloris
in her flimsy veil. Style
and stigma, anthers invite
golden bee to drape itself
in pollen, to crawl toward
ovary atop stiff androgynophore,
feathery corona bed of filament,
petals, sepals, open to joy.

Their green and yellow pods
wrinkle in the light.
Scent drifts across my desk.
I breathe sweetness and sun—
surely Keats's Porphyro

would have strung them
round, on St. Agnes Eve,
placed flower and fruit on soft
pillows to awaken virgin dreams.

No wonder the elders
imposed pain and suffering,
reshaping the floral message,
every delicate part transformed
into blood and cross,
betrayal and guilt—denying
the joy of pure and sensual splendor,
creation and fruition
which surges still.

The Liturgy of Chores

after Degas, Woman Ironing

There is a satisfaction
in pressing metal iron
downward against damp cuff,
working it dry, shaped
flat and smooth—
the angular arm,
the circular motion.

Degas must have seen
that silent power
in the faces at work—
the jutting elbow,
the firm black wedge
wielded over
white collared shirts,
ruffled billowing skirts.

His artist's eye
caught the motion,
the beauty of shifted hip,
bent-back press,
blooming pastel.
All else was secondary—
the laundry stench and heat,
the endless piles of shirt and skirt,
the pallor of women's lives.

I'll take my cue from him—
ignore resentment and sweat,
remember only the touch
of chilled blue cloth,
strength of hand and arm,
that certain twist—push
and press toward rebirth

of rumpled wad and crease
into stiffened collar and sleeve—

then the flattened expanse,
draped downward,
smoothed for badge and tie,
readied with wriggle and point,
the sizzle of blade—
commanding the cloth
as women have done

for centuries—
heating irons on hardened
surfaces, pressing them
to smooth the dampened
Sunday shirts, the weight
of transfiguration
in starch-stiff hands.

Chinaberry Tree

> *Here in this retreat were rest and cool and shelter....*
> *The Chinaberry Tree became a temple.*
> —Jessie Redmon Fauset

i

It's fallen from favor here,
from the days when landscapers
extolled its easy growth—
leaves, shade, delicate flowers
for family lawns. Now the experts
say it's best removed, like expunging
names from country club lists.

Some fearful tribes proclaimed
it the Tree of Knowledge of Good
and Evil, its alluring purple
flowers, bitter bark, tender leaves,
its berry wine. Killing
and uprooting the source
seemed best.

ii

Rumors lived imbedded
in its branches, its bark, its fronds.
Michaux planted chinaberries
by Charleston paths—lush, leafy,
not too tall, shading walkers
from the heat. The "pride of India"
was at home in Southern soil.

Our home sat in the midst
of chinaberry trees, thick and lush.
We named them *umbrella trees*
for their soft rounded tops, their arms
and leaves. I hid in a chinaberry

bower, climbed chinaberry limbs,
swung from a chinaberry tree.

iii
Once, my mother walked me
into the shade, carefully
parted the deep green fronds
like arched bouquets, warning me
not to touch the soft blue thing
nesting there. "Don't ever disturb them.
The mother might leave," she warned.
"Just know they're there."

Once upon a time bluebirds flew
drunken, swaggering, swaying.
They swung and swooped tipsy
on chinaberry wine, sailing
on bird-joy highs—fluffing drunken
feathers on a spring day of nesting,
feasting on green and gold.

My Neighbor Deals with Her Robert E. Lee
Painting

He's riding lean and tall,
galloping through the guest room
saying *Hi-Yo, Traveler,*
this lone ranger of the past,
gentleman of servitude
to grandiose dreams.
Now he's being reined in,
headed for the Swap and Sell.

When the crane swings
him away gently while
he holds his head high,
Traveler never flinches,
his white mane stiff
as an old skull.
Lifted up by a higher power,
he's dangling in the dead air,
moving toward a safe bunker
in the cave of old creeds.

In the Tax Collector's Office

I remember the poll tax books
kept separate according to race,
Black on lower shelves
cause they weren't used much,
Flossie said. Too lazy to pay.

Afternoons in the Neighborhood

Mine were made with town bread, "lightbread"
we called it. My mother stretched margarine
on the pale slice, then sprinkled sugar from
the green glass bowl she'd got in a laundry soap box.
Sometimes, when there was no margarine, a little
dribbled water held the sugar in place.

My brother remembers a leftover biscuit,
buttered, and drizzled with clear-white crystals.
As an old man, he still smiles at that sweet pleasure.
Our neighbor would fix them for all us kids,
our tiny teeth feeling the power crushing
through sugar-crystal granules.

I remember Carol's mother laying out the Sunbeam
slices, portioning the sugar within bread's brown
perimeter while we watched to see what sized heap
we'd get this day. She'd spread it out with a Case knife,
fold the bare half over the drizzled concoction.
She never played favorites though I wasn't her own.

Our mothers bought five-pound bags at Neil's
Grocery. They were too tired to think of rotting
teeth and empty calories. Sugar was cheap.
The steady harvest came in from sweat and blood
in Cuba, as it had come to the Portuguese from Brazil,
as it would come to Americans from Hawaii,

where Queen Liliuokalani would be
deposed and Hawaii Americanized
for sugar. Our mothers were too tired
to worry about human degradation—
they knew only the red, white,
and blue of things.

Within the inexplicable
world, a child might yet taste
sweetness, a makeshift treat,
a gritty morsel, a taste of certainty
shared with circled friends
in sun and shadowed times.

Miss Reese

after Jericho Brown

An olive can take a child to worlds away.
A teacher can prove there's more on Earth than home.

A teacher offers gifts from lands beyond,
a tiny glimpse away from dirt-packed town.

An olive, with toothpick, served to kids from town—
we marveled at its salt, its crunch, its taste.

Some gagged and spewed it out, despised its taste.
Some loved its greenness, savored its salty chew.

Some saw the red dot center, adored its hue.
We learned it came from a boot-shaped foreign place.

Something marvelous came from a foreign place
where sun beat down and olives grew on trees,

where people picked olives growing on knotty trees.
They even had lemons; they spoke in different ways—

lemons and hills, sunshine and long warm days.
An olive can take a child to worlds away.

Ceremonial

When George gave Martha
her fine nuptial bedspread pure white
linen, our mothers were stuffing
cornshucks and straw into sackcloth
and rough cotton, some still sleeping
on bundled rags, dragged toward
somebody's vision of plenitude.

Some were singing of
fine linens and love's betrayal—
How do you like your snow-white
Linens? How do you like your sheet?
How do you like that fair young bride
Laying in your arms asleep—

because even broken-hearted
death was better in a high hall
with soft clean pillows and sheets
than in a straw-stuffed bed in dark cabin.
Our mothers had sung those distant tales,
heard of kingly brocades for royal births.

They knew of fine-wove muslin.
Knew the dream of steady home and hope.
No wonder women knotted, tufted their own
beauties, or settled for plain-sewn
until factory democratized
the bedspread and covered all those layers

barricading from nighttime chill
with purity of tough white cotton
and then chenille, like the one
my mother called counterpane
(after the way of her mother)
which she washed and hung to dry.

It hung so white and thin and worn
you'd think it was witch-spun.
She'd cover that iron bed we slept in,
as chill as the bed of Procrustes,
spread it over layers of worn-stitched
stories from that other life—

smooth white clean—resurfacing
of the bed, always the morning ritual,
the emblem of life's order,
survival out of chaos—always,
until that last morning, the blessed sign
that she would live another day.

After Her Departure

This was the time of no touching.
The one who loved me had died
leaving me tethered to that space
where body had folded into body
assurance that for one night
we were human skin and bones
bound by mysteries unspoken.

She drifted up and I stayed
attached to noise and work
with no threads of oneness
holding me to any other being
on Earth, no reason to justify
the space my body insisted
on shoving itself into
in that place of too little
air and too much mass
knotting itself into a union
a ball, a planet, with me
in its path.

Musicality

How we long for days
of high harmony, each voice
well placed—soprano, alto, tenor,
bass—each voice soaring roofward
in singings, spreading to farm
and village, sending messages
of harmony, no sliding off-key.

No room for those
who could never
find the tune. Ill-fated
destroyers of order,
grownup or child, they
felt the glares of censorship
when they tried to enter in.

No place for those lacking
the tune of whiteness,
notes of stiff Lutherans
and Presbyterians—coal
trains whistled the barrier,
the Great Divide that lingered
after the tracks were uprooted.

That lingers still—
joggers run shining in Under
Armour shorts. Pale fathers
push their babies who snuggle
in blankets, tucked in smooth-
wheeled strollers, the concrete
walkway an easy ride.

Oatmeal

When I was a child my mother
cooked oatmeal for my breakfast
every day. She'd fire up that wood-
burning stove, load the kettle
with water, add it to the oatmeal pot,
stir in the dry oats, and let them slow
cook while I dressed for school
by the coal-warmed stove.

"Oatmeal sticks to the bones,"
she'd say, as her mother had said
to her. She'd allow a little sugar,
a tiny bit of cream. I never questioned
or begged for more sweetness,
more creamy delight, but bowed
my head, said my blessing,
and dived into the warmth.

Grandmother had eaten her
share of oats back in the shack
of her childhood, where
her days were spent
hoeing her uncle's corn
in the glare of Alexander
County red clay fields,
no time for school.

Not all that different
from those ancient Morrison
kin she'd heard of, the great-
grandfathers and uncles who
came from Scotland through Ireland
to farm this land on the backs
of lifelong slaves and poor kin.
Such poverty-tainted food—

you'd think it might carry
a bitter taste from all those years
of history. Instead, it spoke
of fortitude and dreams, survival,
salvation. No wonder my mother
insisted upon bowed heads chanting
rhymes, a liturgy of gratitude,
the sustaining grain, the wafer of life.

Hog Pen Seasons

When we were neighbor-young
and dirty in a pack wild-running-
squealing for something to do besides
play checkers and make cookies,
our mothers made us go outside
where we could do no harm

to antimacassars and Sunday pies.
We'd find solace down past mowed-
grass boundaries at the Jordans' pigpen
where the hollyhocks grew tall and lush—
pink, purple, and white—
while the mud-caked hogs

wallowed in the summer heat.
We didn't mind the smell of slop and scat.
Maybe we were a little jealous,
not knowing what to do while
the hogs grunted with sleepy pleasure,
unconcerned about their own fate.

The scalding tubs sat grounded in the barn,
the pulleys ready for hanging hoofs,
the trappings cleaned for pink slick guts.
A bucket of scraps and a garbage-filled
trough brought lazy slobbers and oinks.
And when the aroma of pigpen came to drift

in the chilly gust, suddenly another wallow
and grunt—then the blinding slash—
bloody entrails curled in an old tin pail,
no steaming message left for man or beast—
no visit from the gods, no thunder
against greed and sloth.

Home Economics

Miss Miller told us
>	we needed girdles
>	like she needed a good drink.

She didn't actually say anything about the drink
>	but we smelled it
>	among the biscuits
>	and baked bananas.

Without girdles, she said,
>	our bony thighs would not lie smooth and tamed,
>	our teenaged bellies would swell and sag.
>	She breathed an unspoken fear.

We might venture beyond the rules.
>	And once a body yields
>	to pleasures outside the zone
>	there is no salvation.

The only choice becomes
>	the tedium of the molten hours.
>	The drowning in the dark.

Pinto Beans

Consider the lowly beans—
not Jack's beans of course,
leading to goose's golden eggs
and evil giants. No—think
of the beans your mother
worked through to pick out the rocks,
lest you break a tooth in the devouring
of her near-daily supper, the bagged

little spotted ones, the cheapest
and most familiar, most comforting—
the ones your grandmother loved.
When they simmer, you recognize
the smell. It's a comfort smell.
Now you want chow-chow,
maybe onions, maybe a little ketchup.

It wasn't always like that,
this soothing easy aroma
that meant you wouldn't starve,
meant you might have cornbread,
even a little margarine.
Now they're easy to forget,
these pintos still stacked

in plastic bags on grocery shelves.
After all, the lentils tempt,
an array of colors—the tiny yellow,
green, red, brown—a touch
of the exotic, and now, bags of little beans,
some black, some green, some white.
There's fashion in beans.

We've improved our pintos
from their deep viney origins within

the mountains of South America. They
stand, officially registered, upright
for easy picking, though it took
some breeding and inbreeding
to bring them under control.

Five thousand years of pintos, they say,
to get to this point, upward from Peru,
through the Andes, the North, the great
American Southwest, onward, moving
across the ocean to Europe and back.
Pintos travel well, are easy to carry along,
easy to grow, easy to cook, to eat.

Some refried them into paste,
some added meat, chili,
some added extra water, called
them *soup beans*. Poverty encourages
stretching the beans. Consider
the beans that kept you alive
when all else was shambles.

Remember your mother's hands,
how they sorted and shelled the rocks
and trash, soaked,
washed and cooked,
and cooked and cooked for hours
without burning,
without wasting a bit.

II.

It is true, I never assisted the sun materially in his rising, but doubt not, it was of the last importance only to be present at it.

—Henry David Thoreau

Years

I have no excuse for staying this long
beyond the sheer joy of soft breeze,
the distant roar of trucks, the yellow
swallowtail drifting by, seeking nectar
for its short duration. Like me,
sipping the nectar of life till lips
are cracked and dry like late
summer swallowtail wings, like
Mother Mary's must have been,
or the Queen's after all those long years.

Black Swallowtail, New Birthed

On the floor the stain of frass,
pale green, from her caterpillar body
as she pulsated near-dry—
soft, black, yellow, white—
still frail against wasp panzer
destroyer—spared only
by protective screen.

She had crawled, pupated,
thrown out her silken anchor,
spun two threads, hardened
fragile skin to chrysalis.
What's left hangs on a rough serrated leaf—
jagged open where she broke through,
dragged her weighted wings, crawled
free, pumped velvet blue-black.

Now she dances against the screen.
       An open door and she's free!
       Leaves us stuck on concrete
       aglow with pleasure at her flight.

Philosophers speak of
ancient China, of butterflies
and man's burden, of time,
the Great Zhuangzi and his dreams
of weightlessness, freedom,
a different reality.
       We watch communion
       between butterfly and flower,
       a brevity of touch,
           a sharing—
       hold tight
       to ticking clock.

Stitching

My mother was a good girl—she saved
her baby thimble, kept her sewing basket near
her rocking chair—in case of a moment
of leisure. They all stitched, women of that time

and place—mended, made lace,
crocheted little doilies, embroidered,
for beauty, virtue, for ticking off the hours.
My mother lived in a small plank house,

holding us close on poverty's slickened cliff.
Needles were for repairs—letting out
hems and sleeves for next year's wear.
And yet, implements for beauty, for quilting,

embroidery, elevating the plainness of life,
imbedding platitudes in messages of thread.
Mothers, grandmothers, unknown shapes and faces,
strained at the bare fibers of histories untold.

If you hold her small dark thimble
to the light, look deep inside. You'll see
a tiny point of bright where the metal collapsed,
the needlehead punched into tender skin.

You'll need a lens to see the message
beneath the thimble rim, words inscribed,
too small to read in tarnished darkness—
    "For a Good Girl."

Hers was a time when worth was measured
in stitches, when straight and tiny
were codes for virtue—small stitches,
small steps, no careless expectations.

The culture of thimbles pulsates
through continents, through eons.
Ancient tapestries beautify glories
of conquerors, kings, and queens,

stitched by ladies of virtuous renown.
Cave dwellers, mammoth hunters
living within the edge of extinction
decorated their hides with pearls.

My mother, not far removed
from such raw survival, pierced
the rough hide of her life,
stitching pearls along the way.

What We Carry

I thought of Proust today,
the smell of vanilla,
the perfect molded palmate,
its edge dipped in tea.

I thought of Robert Burns,
born on a short dark plank,
forever shadowed,
regardless of sunburnt arms.

I thought of you, hiding,
waiting for the moment
of small boy joy. The father
swills a drink in the garage.

That lightning throat burned
into your childheart
in flames that will not
be contained.

Translucent

They gave me the tiny dresser,
as if one little piece crafted by him
from leftover factory wood
would somehow help me know,
a molecular fusion of sorts from his hands
to my infant grasping fingers,
those he held in the last days
before his death, tiny hands
wrapped around his bony fingers,
joints shining through
blue translucent skin.

Saturdays

> *Bill Haley's recording became an anthem for rebellion for 1950s youth.*
> —Deena Weinstein

I did the diapers—swished
them shit-free, dumped them
from pail to machine. I slipped
to the clothesline, hung them
to dry, folded them for fit.

I stacked the dishes
by the sink—washed
dried, shelved, wiped
the counters clean while
the radio sifted songs, sizzled.

Bill Haley came through,
muttered his advice—
too soft for the family to hear.
"Rock around the clock," he said.
"Rock around the clock tonight."

Spider Lilies

Deep red threads hover
foreign, uninvited, skinny,
not the soft comfort of daisy and rose.
Against the grass they sprout scarlet
while all else prepares for winter's rest.
Tall thin petals stand
above our close-cropped lawn,
mystical, leafless.

They come from lands
where gods float cloudy
beyond our definition—
brought west to Carolina
by Perry's men, emblems
of the unknown, like magic
from celestial skies.
"Flowers of the heavens,"
they carry both life and death.
In Japanese gardens they grow
thick—their blooms, nuzzle cozy,
fill in the leafless void.
Mourners lay them on graves.

On the lawn they grow
sparse, naked, stiff
in the chill, in lonely
baldness, an alien curiosity.
We're warned not to touch,
not to breathe the floral scent,
which will sicken a rabbit or squirrel.
Long-legged stamens evoke
some faint scent of exotic
death in fragile petals,
red, stalk-naked stringy, dangling
like unleashed spider legs
suspended before the jump.

Faucet

Our old faucet fell off,
    its plastic part, built
        for easy destruction,
landed with a soft plop.

Our new faucet
    is tall and curved,
        smooth and promising
in its brushed chrome beauty.

My mother kept our water
    on the porch
        in two white red-rimmed buckets,
a dipper always within reach.

My brother's task
    was to keep the two
        filled from the backyard well.
That was easy—dip the wooden bucket,

pour the pure cold chill
    into enameled metal,
        listen to its song.
Not like the old place, where she

clambered down a muddy
    bank to bring up water
        in battered buckets—
their thin-wire handles digging into skin.

It must have been a salvation of sorts—
    step outside,
        drop a bucket, water
for the beans she was cooking,

water for thirsty kids,
>   water for washtub baths.
>   >   I remember the tub hanging
on the house side, outside the kitchen,

what it meant,
>   the folded-up child body-bath,
>   >   the scrubbing of shirts
against ridged metal.

What labor water commands!
>   I have seen women balance
>   >   tall jugs on slim necks,
vertebrae sinking deeper day by day.

I've seen it delivered in wagons, to refugees
>   camped in deserts—
>   >   >   channeled through lead pipes
which eat away the brains of children.

I've seen the white-robed baptizers,
>   the total trust
>   >   required for immersion.
I think of the woman at Jacob's well.

Is a dry throat
>   moistened with words?
>   >   When He offered the Water
of Life, did she drink from the cup?

My Brother Takes a Paper Route

When he was nine years old
my brother delivered papers
to both sides of town.

The names of
streets during the war years
—Rumple, Brown, Sherrill—

roll off his eighty-four-
year-old tongue as if
he still delivered those stories

of failings and successes,
the war news, obituaries.
He drives slow,

hardening boy-thin arms,
pushing that heavy bike, his
sister's girl-bike from a past age.

He pauses still to make his throw,
remembers the divide across the tracks
where women saw his plight

on rainy days, protected him
for his mother as best they could,
all hovered in darkness
beneath a southern sky.

Winter Studies

Consider the small drab sparrow,
its beating heart,
its brown plainness
designed to save
its tiny body
from mighty hawk.
And yet the cycle commands.

Once I sat quiet, sparrow
feeding at my side—
hawk swooped,
clutched bird
with mighty claws.
My heart beat hard,
sought comfort words.

No room for explication—
soft brown sparrows feast
beside bright bluebirds
with rosy chests
and feather-white bellies.
On the grass below, doves
search, feed on crumbs.

Warped

Her quilting frames lie gray
suspended upon the front porch rafters
of the house where I was born, the house
that I don't own, bought by some stranger
for the value of land, a man who knows nothing
of the breath of life that lingers in an old house
where generations were born and died,
the lingering music of old prayers.

In that small front room where the frames
were raised to the ceiling to be unnoticed,
like so much of women's work,
tucked away while meals were cooked, sheets
were washed, housedresses were whipped together
from flour sacks, the humdrum labor of cooking beans
and washing bedsheets, women
pieced mismatched crazy quilts out of old scraps.

Then somebody said there's enough here to make
butterflies. We'll share scraps, make one for the both of us,
stitching together and setting up those old frames
from Grandmother's day when she aimed only for warmth—
we'll measure, stripe, and stitch for butterfly squares
all thirty-eight flying toward that purple morning glory
in the center they'd be drawn to, the sweet scent of glory
luring them inward from all directions
to whatever pleasures might be wrested
from the work of survival.

Now Walmart and Penney's sell factory quilts
and fluffy blankets with far less cost
than such things can be made
at home. And who feels
like quilting after a long day
in class, at the mill, in the office?

So the frames remained
at the old house, grayed
and warped. Their wood
lying there longer than
my grandmother has been dead,
longer than my mother
has been lying in her grave.

Old Women Passing Time

On Saturday nights they played cards—
setback—they'd played it all their lives.
They were three leftovers from glory days
when the valley teamed with fertility.
Nelle, Mary Ellen, and Bea—two widows
and the spinster aunt living in small white houses
dotted among fields now rented for hay.
They came to Nelle's house—she'd never
learned to drive, and that big fireplace
warmed old bones. Ignoring the maple table,
bearer of old pride, they dragged out the shaky
card table and straight-backed chairs.

Then they played, cheating freely.
Somebody would gently pull up the corner
of a face-down card while the other two
studied the light bulbs or got some tea.
Why not? They'd practiced not noticing
late-night absences, frivolous pleasures of males,
the lonely drunken bouts of men they loved.
Old age may bring its glory days. They
had grieved, come undone from duties.
This is what was left, the single-digit years—
the putting away of old suffering, the silliness of play,
a game nobody has to win, a quietude.

Thanksgiving Day

The last time I saw him
he was standing in the hall
not quite hearing what we said
not quite seeing us try to smile
not quite knowing where or who he was

so he said what he knew to say:
Thank you for coming over
We enjoyed having you
Be careful driving home
Come back anytime

Morning in the Cove

The fog wraps its pale fist
        around gold-tipped beech,
burnished oak, rusty yellows of walnut
        leaves, the thousand firebushes,
red as their name, all spread
        in brambled confusion
by jagged damp creek.

Too much joy so sudden
        might burst beyond the heart's
capacity. So slowly
        she sheds the gray gloves,
releases fading fingers to plowed field,
        gives over to brightness and glory
almost too brilliant to bear.

Searching for My Brother

In the winter that he died,
old, tired, half-sensing he'd been cheated,
I tried to write him understandable.
He'd been a kid who watched our father
drop muscle and fat, turn walking skeleton,
collapse within the house while his son tried
to be six years old for those moments his daddy
could take him fishing, briefly alive with morphine.

"I ain't the baby no more," he said
when I was born. But joy was quickly
replaced with grief for lost
childhood silliness
amidst all that new birth
and death
leaving no time nor space for
one small boy.

So he hid under the rock-raised house,
shadowed in the cool dark dirt
while they searched and called his name,
beloved little trickster, tousled and curly
who'd known nothing of pain and death
and being replaced.

In a few weeks he'd be held high
to watch his father die to the
murmurings of the Lord's Prayer.
Lonely boy of chaos severed from
childhood's clouds of glory
into the iron claws of loss
that never released him
even as he pulled himself
upward into adulthood against the clang
and pound of relentless memory.

At the end, they left him
alone in a sterile bed,
where he called out to the nurses
for his own kin, lost brother,
the lost father of his childhood
for footballs and new bikes,
those last days of overalls
and hayfields and romping cousins
within the pearly dawn of life.

Spawning Fish Against the Dam

On this April day
when the laurel is in bloom

and moist chicks
wiggle in their eggs,

restless shad
lunge at concrete slabs

sink down
in sterile waters

muddied
by their own wounds.

First Iris

These deep purples always take me
to my mother. She'd brought them with her
to this shabby shack of a house
with no history to hold it up like the deep-
walled cabin that had held her life together,
rich with old logs to hold the planks,
added later mostly for show.

The irises blazed prosperity
and leisure, time for beauty,
beside the firebush and fig.
Some rhizomes bloomed around back
perhaps because of careless toss,
that purple splashing all around.
She'd tried to save a few reminders.

All buried in the ground—
father, husband, mother too.
No wonder our Easter eggs
held the deepest royal glow
always glossed with Crisco,
flaunting that purple sheen she'd never dare
to wear, in her widow's mournful black.

III.

…because the light clinging to the window is at its most reflective / just as it is ready to go out.

—Linda Pastan

Royal Purple

My mother
dug up rhizomes from the family farm,
carried them to the shabby shack
where we had moved.
My small face buried itself
among the blossoms.
I breathed deep rooty sweetness.

Our teacher taught us to draw them.
Every child succeeded, the petals delicate,
the falls rich, the brush golden. Later,
we could sit down, feel
Miss Allison's guiding hand,
lay down on paper the purple iris
of childhood.

We carry its rhizomes
home to home,
from somebody's grandmother,
somebody's dear friend,
the deep purple, peach,
lavender.

Our forebears pounded,
ground, sifted its roots—powdered
its flour into stiffened hair, rubbed it
into woolen clothing,
tried to capture its scented glory,
boiled rhizomes with linens
for its sweet smell.

In ancient times,
Iris was messenger of the gods
on Earth. The spirits
of noble women followed her

to Elysian Fields. Royal purples
bloomed on their graves.
Some kinship hints its existence.

Sometimes, away from tended
lawns, a gentle surprise—
the small sweet flag
of iris gone wild
in swamp or on mountain,
its little blue flags like whispered
messages from Olympus.

Duplex for Junk Mail

after Jericho Brown

We know our grief by things our loved ones touched.
A chance discovery might erase all time.

      Chance brings unwanted leaps through time.
      A *Reader's Digest* lies among the junk-mail trash.

I see her sitting in her appointed place,
holding to her page with fragile hand.

      Her *Digest* always there beside her hand,
      her fragile heart ticking off the days.

A child cannot conceive of death's cold ways,
fails to understand the heart's thin pace.

      I brought her tea, sat down beside her place.
      She smiled while listening to my schoolgirl talk.

On that last day she listened while I talked.
We know our grief by things our loved ones touched.

Sunday Evening

Across the street the yellow machines
are done with grinding the orange gash
where the stray cat once lived among
luscious weeds, mice, and moles.

They'll come back with heavy-bodied
packers, meant to pound every modicum
of living earth for concrete slab to be poured,
rectangulated into a house much like my own.

Another red clay pasture lies north
on Old Mountain Road—two more south,
on Perth. The green of home is blotted
with orange swaths and giant yellow bugs.

This earth is veined with asphalt roads opening
into clay acres, hectares. In Brazil slaughtered trees
are repurposed into logging planks, the barren gaps
seeded with crops—perhaps bananas, oil palm, or tea.

I've been to England, photographed green round hills
and gardened cottages where forests once
grew tall. I've seen America's lakes shrinking
distant from dried-out piers and boat-launch pads.

We are in Earth's gloaming, beauteous
sunsets of red-rolled dust. We soothe ourselves
with green-turfed fields, bright screens
filled with fantasy to dull the sound of grind.

Here we do our part—feed the hummingbirds,
grow milkweed and parsley for butterflies,
nibble the golden crust of apple fritters,
wait for some Power to call *ENOUGH*!

Photo of Boy and Dog: Triptych

The dog holds out his paw,
fuzzy in the photo, but waiting
to be held. The boy's hand
is near the paw, his other hand
wrapped around the dog,
Fixate on hand and paw,
human—doggy nails
so close, for joy, not pain.
This is dog-love, boy-love—
as close to oneness as two species
can get. Bodies lean into love.
All centers on paw and hand
near each other, trying to hold on.

It's an old snapshot,
black and white.
No artsy composition,
just grab the boy and dog
together. It's been scanned,
enlarged from a tiny 4x3,
imperfections heightened.
The white blemish at the boy's temple,
bright against his tanned face,
white and black streaks trailing
downward, maybe from the printer.
The photographer probably didn't mean
to capture that gray downward
pointing cluster of leaves,
hovering above boy and dog,
the outbuilding with invisible
roof. He probably had to act fast,
before they disappeared.

This isn't the photo I remember—
Here is cozy boy-dog love.

You can see how the boy's eyes
stare straight down—a heart-gaze.
Not too long from now,
the neighbor will poison the dog.
The picture I remember is the boy
walking out of the woods, carrying
the dog like a baby. It is dying.
The boy heaves his last gasp
of childhood.

Ghazal for the Lost

On this darkened day, the soul abjures belief.
The wet and rotting rain on graves calls out for grief.

With frail and pleasant scents we structure barricades
built of pies and cakes and fruits for the bereft.

He was the quiet brother, spoke with paint and wood.
When his heart exploded, we were amazed by grief.

She sewed and hemmed, wrought beauteous gifts from scraps.
She garnered chaos, tidied life by seam and stitch.

He could not say goodbye but offered gifts instead.
His teasing left him voiceless, inept at speaking grief.

You—brother, sister, brother—dissolved in death.
The rotting rain on lonely graves calls out my grief.

Surfacing the Swamp

I watch the darkening landscape
enshrouding hummocks and trees.
Stars glow blue-white in this dark
place. Constellations proclaim their stories
against the blackness while tree frogs
sing a bass chorus. Owls hoot softly,
not for us,
inviting endless flutter among bare-
limbed cypress draped with lacy moss.

Today the ibis convene on old limbs,
their beaks in curving conversation.
Dragonflies hover midair in pairs,
if ever two were one, they are—
some brown, some striped, some
sky-blue bodies held up by black-
lace pairs of gauzy wings. Turtles sit
on favorite logs above their mirrored selves
in burnished Suwannee waters.

The gators have grown gigantic, faking
ferocity, but they don't really care.
We stay our distance while they
occasionally open lidded eyes,
slow and ancient and aware, smiling
their message of deep waters.

For an Unknown Father

A photo father on a cliff wears shiny shoes.
Sometimes we mourn the loss of those we never knew.

They tell me how he stooped and cried when I was born.
A quarter in my piggy bank was all I knew.

His restless spirit sometimes led to curse and blame.
Tied to plow and farm and child, he felt subdued.

He loved the push of wind, the breeze of biking roads,
bought his children the best of bikes, all shining new.

He hoisted the latest kid, took him to corner stores.
Not me, of course. He died before I ever knew.

A mountain-loving man in shining shoes—
sometimes I mourn the loss of one I never knew.

Road

We are lost within a twilight dust
peering through a gate at stiffened men
standing pale on porches made of screen
tacked to trailers streaked by trails of rust.
Bare bulbs from ceilings light up moth and dust
down the row of naked lights between
the bikes and trikes and clothesline strings.
The residue of days rolls in the mist.
We're stranded here in winter's waning light
outside a ring of pale and shadowed men.
What awful turn led to this lonely sight,
this foggy porch-lit pattern at day's end?
Turn away from jagged jaws and dirt.
Roll on to easy light and urban scene.

Lake Walk in January

All the neutral shades of the universe
are mottled on this ground where we
shamble about through winter's decay,
the pines too frozen to offer their usual pitch.
Some stand dying, patches bare of bark
where the beavers chewed last spring.
The only sound's a distant plane,
a human shuffling of chilled boots
far distant from Earth's warm core.

Then the great blue heron squawks,
a comic protest belittling his majesty.
We are too near his fishing spot,
so he chooses another rock on lake bank
safe from humans, stares beneath the water,
spears a silver fish, works it off his beak,
tosses it down his throat, stares again.
He misses the next one, long gray neck
shakes off chill water, his eye once more focused,
but we are too impatient to wait.

I think of those points south
where egrets and herons share sunshine
and swimming schools, wade in lush grasses,
their warm legs wet within a feast of options
station themselves at respectful distances—
little green, tri-color, yellow-headed night
and little blue, great egret, ibis, great blue—
chatting amiably, working out the details.
A gracious plenty in the water,
flowing pastures of heaven
where the sun sets late in the evening—
herons settle on plush hummocks
near their neighbors, squawking softly,
with full bellies and easy accord.

Instructions for a Winter Day

Give thanks
to the unknown Power
baptizing our Earth
with the rain of life
on this drear day.

Sing Halleluiah
to the Gods of every
name—for red clay puddles
and doves bobbing
in rooty blades,

for voices beneath
the grass, where all things
churn and whisper *new worms*
new roots, old roots
sanctified.

About the Old Jesus Print Propped Up Behind the Chest in My Bedroom

after Josef Untersberger (Giovanni), Christ the Shepherd

Every time I think I'll carry it
to the thrift store, I see
my grandmother shake her head,
my father stare at that gentle Jesus
looking for some sign of hope
while Jesus holds the lamb,
lets the sheep nibble at his knees.

It hung over the fireplace in that old
family house inundated with death and sorrow,
above the beds of the dying, the beloved.
It's a small thing, this holding of lambs,
this propping up of faith in death's despair.
Why can't I give it over, this bargain
some needful soul might yet find
in a dusty aisle loaded with life's sorrows?

Pompeii

It's not the rich man
I remember most, stretched
on his leisure couch,
caught sleeping—not
the housewife, or servant,
bending over the oven
checking on her baking bread.
It's not even the sex slaves.

The murals have lost their glow,
faded and cracked, on the walls
of wealthy men who hung
around in easy togas,
near their fine baths
where they soaked
and chatted at leisure, their
wine jugs now piled in corners.

It's the little dog—
sleek, legs bowed, tense,
claws tight, maybe barking
at the red-ash rush that
ate him while he was just
being a dog in the street,
looking for a handout maybe,
a toss of hard bread,
a pat on the head.

Butterfly Weed

Tough little wild dig
from the mountain neighbor's
rutty road. We'd stolen it
since he wasn't there to care,
brought it down drooping
near death, but by the time
the caterpillars were feeding
it had bloomed orange and stiff
ready to cradle those pupae
who hadn't been devoured by wasps,
nursery to monarch unfolding its wings
to those few weeks of beauty
untouched by self-awareness,
free from constant reminders
of past and future.

Monuments

Knowing of Odysseus
and Paris, the great Alexander,
Charlemagne, and William,
we chose our own heroes,
held fast to precious myths,
planted magnolias, carved
outsized statues of marble
and bronze. Now they twist
in troubled times, swing like
corpses left on limbs.
We nurse the aching tooth
that cannot be absolved
until its bloody extraction.

Apology to Ralph's Mule

> *...and before them went the mules: and ever upward,*
> *downward, sideward, and aslant they fared.*
> —*The Iliad* II.23.93

You stood there in mud and dung,
your little streetside lot hardly big enough
for a good stretch, a kick.
I'd stop sometimes, Ralph's Mule,
think about the muck on your hooves,
how it must feel, you standing
in the mud, mired in that nasty mess.

I never knew your name.
Your owner was a silhouette at church.
He sometimes walked behind you
in his field, making mule noises—
gee and haw, some throaty cluck. You
obeyed, walked the straight line,
turned, walked back.

I never spoke to you then.
Now I like to dream your mule-brain
felt the glories of your kind,
not mired down in one dull field,
hitched to one dull man—no mule friends,
alone, bored in your tiny lot.
I'd like to think you found

some collective memory, Ralph's Mule—
such as humans seek. You showed
up in movies. John Wayne had *Jeanette*,
the Waltons their *Blue*. Sometimes
you conversed. Twenty of you brought borax
from the deep western desert to my house.
Our old sheets were dazzle white!

We didn't know you'd worked
the battlefields of ancient Grecian Wars—
bled, died, were devoured as you are today.
Your image is imbedded in Assyrian murals,
in ancient stories of human woe. You died
among the bombs in our grim battles,
slaughtered by both sides.

You're in old photographs of Carolina farmers,
their fields and wagons, their teams, names
scrawled on the backs. You're in cities where
lonely lots once stood, where townsmen
played out lost lives. You stood your ground,
the burden of your kind
ignored by the likes of us.

My Mother Digs Up Irises When She Moves

They won't keep quiet, these flowers
of my childhood that have bloomed
for generations of mothers and daughters.
My mother dragged them to a shabby house
she'd bought to spare her kids the farmhand life,
embedded irises beside the window,
next to her sleeping place.
Every year they speak of what she lost
and what she saved, these blooms, royal purple,
rich and golden in the center,
lush in this new soil of grief and hope.

Eclipse with Bees

Sit in the quiet grass,
watch a gathering hive
beneath the darkening sky
on a summer afternoon.
A soft whirr says peace and purpose
as bees drop to bottom board,
orange and gold packed tight
between body and dangling legs,

their load balanced
to make it bearable.
Stomachs filled with nectar,
pollen for bee bread, they crawl home
where the queen is laying eggs.
Sniff the aroma of the hive,
the racks where she
scurries on waxy cells,

creates beginnings
for worker bees,
lazy drones, perhaps a queen
to supplant her. Breathe that life smell—
somehow musty and floral,
slightly sweet. Feel the soft song
rolling smooth order
within the dark.

Humankind has long shaped
hives of log and clay
mud and straw, harvested honey
in jugs, answered bees'
sweet purr with holy drone,
hymn of praise, the stuff of light—
beeswax, candles
held in sacred ceremony.

Watch as darkness withdraws,
daylight opens, bees return
in studied order, obey
the rhythm that triggers—
day and dark
and dark and day again,
gives voice to ancient
hymn once droned

from hollowed tree,
crevice of craggy cliff,
baskets woven in Africa,
clay pots filled with harvest,
the pleasure of honey and cheese in Pompeii.
Now, in the quiet grass, a backyard box
racked and filled with wax and honey,
feel the countermelodies, the hum of holiness.

Watching the Rain

Goldfinch and hummingbird,
the shabby cardinal all hover
in adolescent attire.

Sparrows make love
on the birdhouse roof,
go inside

translate passion
into eggs
of commitment.

Fecundity abounds.
I offer back porch
benediction.

Last Light

The leaf-light sifts
translucent burnished red
against the green
and yellow maple
through the screen filter
of my porch
illuminating the frail
and certain paths
the shiny silver stories
of patience and questing
in the dark and shrouded night
when moths fly in twilight's
shadow, compelled and unafraid.

Notes

"In the Tax Collector's Office." Begun in the 1890s as a legal way to keep African Americans from voting, five states enforced payment of poll taxes for state elections until 1966, when the U.S. Supreme Court declared them unconstitutional.

"Ceremonial" incorporates "Little Margaret," Child Ballad #74. Francis Child, *English and Scottish Ballads*, in Sargent, Helen Child, and George Lyman Kittredge, eds. 1904.

Acknowledgments

The author thanks the following publications for recognition of the poems listed below and published with some possible slight changes.

County Lines: "Duplex for Junk Mail," "Old Women Passing Time"
Dead Mule School of Southern Poetry: "First Iris," "The Jesus Print"
Ephemeral Elegies: "Photo of Boy and Dog"
Front Porch Review: "A Slow Unpacking"
Galway Review: "Last Light"
Main Street Rag: "Home Economics"
North Carolina Literary Review: "Chinaberry Tree," "Stitching"
Pine Mountain Sand & Gravel: "Translucent"
Pinesong: "Ghazal for the Lost"
Reedy Branch Review: "Iris," "Miss Reese," "Surfacing the Swamp"
Salvation South: "My Mother Digs Up Irises When She Moves"
Still: The Journal: "Ceremonial," "The Liturgy of Chores"
Streetlight: "Passionflowers," "Apology to Ralph's Mule"

The author thanks the sponsors of contests that recognized the following poems: "Duplex for Junk Mail" and "Old Women Passing Time" (Franklin County Arts Council Carolina Writers Contest, honorable mention); "Pinto Beans" (North Carolina Poetry Society, Poet Laureate finalist); "Ghazal for the Lost" (Joanna Catherine Scott Award, honorable mention); "Chinaberry Tree" and "Stitching" (*North Carolina Literary Review*, James Applewhite finalists); and "Apology to Ralph's Mule" (*Streetlight*, 2023 Poetry Contest third place winner).

Deep gratitude to Pauletta Hansel—master poet, teacher, editor—for her boundless help in bringing this book to fruition. From the beginning, my decision to enroll in her manuscript course not only brought forth a stronger text, but an improved skill in developing, rethinking, and improving an initial piece until honed beyond its original existence into a finer document reflecting the poet's unknown possibilities. Without Pauletta's gentle nudging toward its highest standard, this manuscript would not have reached its highest potential.

The fine and demanding eye of extraordinary poet and Madville poetry editor Linda Parsons brought this book to realization on a higher plane than I had foreseen possible. Her powerful perception and skill moved the text to polished fruition. As an early admirer of Madville Publishing when it was founded by Kim Davis, director, I am honored to become one of the authors whose works found their intellectual and spiritual home in Madville.

About the Author

Joyce Compton Brown was born into an agrarian German/Scots-Irish farm family in Iredell County, North Carolina. Appalachian State University confirmed her love for the mountains and Appalachian music, where she took classes in the Child Ballads and other subjects under the founder of the Appalachian Studies Association, Cratis Williams, and acquired her first banjo. Between bouts of paper grading at Gardner-Webb University, she welcomed chances to learn at Berea College and Hindman Settlement School writing workshops. Her early writing focuses on her Southern family roots and stories she heard as a child. Later writing, though based in specificity, strives for a sense of universality. She is the author of four previous books of poetry, most recently *Hard-Packet Clay*.

www.ingramcontent.com/pod-product-compliance
Lightning Source LLC
Chambersburg PA
CBHW031607110426
42742CB00037B/1323